DIY
fairy gardens

5 UNIQUE PROJECTS for
HOME DÉCOR MAGIC

LEISURE ARTS, INC. • Maumelle, Arkansas

Welcome to the world of fairy gardens! It's small yet packed with design! Each enchanting garden is fun to customize and make your own. Have fun making a rope hut, tire swing, fire pit, hammock, trellis, bridge and more! This book is suitable for adults and children and the fun can go on for hours when you make-believe!

table of contents

beach garden

Surf's up! Bring back memories of the beach with an indoor beach garden. All the elements are here and you can customize the hammock and surf board colors. The garden is created in several steps; just follow along with the photos. Kowabunga dude!

SHOPPING LIST

Layering Materials

- [ ] Glass container (my container is 6¼" square and 7½" high)
- [ ] 3 – 1.5 lb. bottles of sand (light brown, dark brown, white)
- [ ] Driftwood (I used 4 pieces about 4½" long and ½" diameter)
- [ ] Shells
- [ ] River rocks
- [ ] Multicolored mini pebbles
- [ ] Disposable plastic water bottle
- [ ] Faux plants

Hammock

- [ ] 2" x 3" piece of fabric
- [ ] Cotton cording: 4 pieces cut at 7" long each
- [ ] 2 – 6" twigs for supports
- [ ] 4 – 3½" x ¼" craft wood picks, cut into 1½" pieces

Surfboard & Beach Ball

- [ ] Oven bake polymer clay (any color since it will be painted)
- [ ] Acrylic paint in desired colors
- [ ] Clay rolling pin
- [ ] Clay cutting tool

Travel Sign

- [ ] Acrylic paint in desired colors
- [ ] 3 – 3½" x ¼" craft wood picks
- [ ] Permanent pen

General Supplies

- [ ] Hot glue and glue gun
- [ ] Paintbrushes
- [ ] Craft knife

TO MAKE THE BEACH GARDEN:

Layering

1. Cut the water bottle.

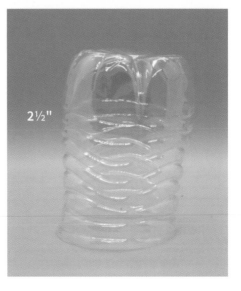

2. Place driftwood pieces, river rocks and cut water bottle in container. Fill bottle with rocks.

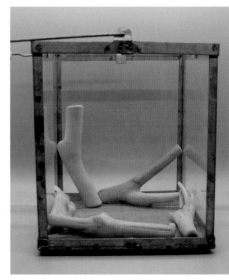

3. Layer the 2 darker colors of sand in the container, creating dips and waves with sand. Add some mini pebbles around the edges so they show through the glass. Keep adding sand and pebbles until the layers are even with the cut water bottle. Add a few more river rocks. Top with a layer of white sand.

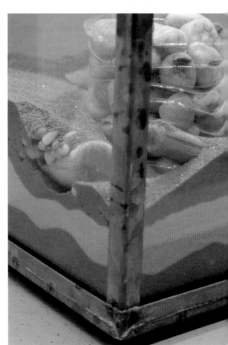

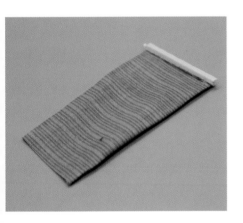  

Hammock

1. Glue long edges of fabric ¼" to the back.

2. Glue 1 wood pick to one short edge. Glue 2 cording ends to back of hammock on edge with pick. Glue 1 wood pick over the cording ends. Repeat on opposite short edge.

3. Tie cording ends together in a knot 1" from the short edges.

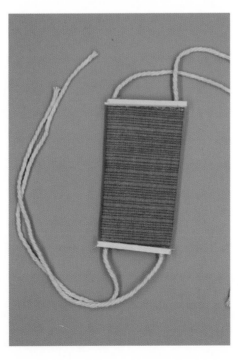 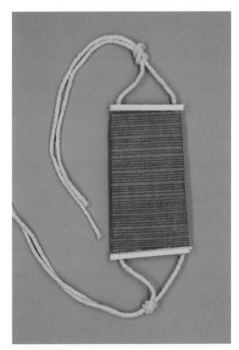

Travel Sign

1. Break 2 of the wood picks in half, leaving rough edges.

2. Paint the broken picks. Use the permanent pen to add words and arrows to painted picks. I suggest Beach, Trail, Park and Camp.

3. Glue painted picks on remaining unpainted pick.

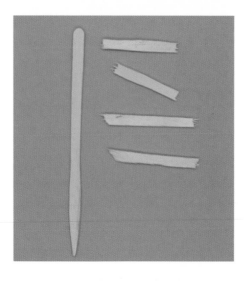

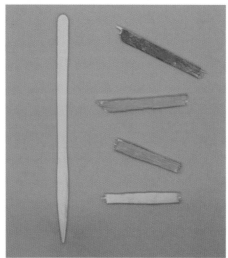

Surfboard & Beach Ball

1. Knead clay until it is soft and pliable.

2. For the surfboard, roll the clay to ¼" thick. Cut out a surfboard shape that is about 3¾" long and 1¼" wide. Use your fingers to smooth the cut edges.

3. For the beach ball, roll the clay into 1" ball.

4. Follow the manufacturer's instructions to bake the clay pieces; let cool. Paint as desired.

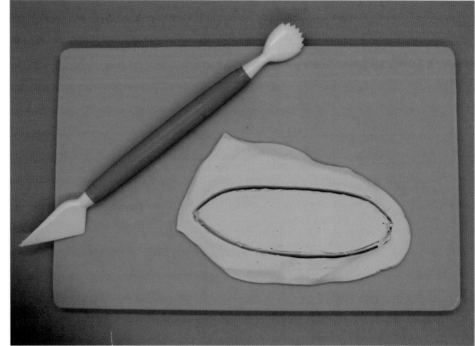

Assembly

Add the plants to the container, gently moving the sand, rocks and pebbles as needed. Insert the hammock support twigs in the sand; tie the cording around the twigs and trim the ends. Add the travel sign, surfboard and beach ball. Fill in with white sand, pebbles, shells and rocks as desired.

rose hut garden

Fairies are proud of their gardening skills and are delighted to welcome vistors with open arms. Enjoy the breezy swing amongst the succulents and flowers or take a leisurely nap in the organic rose-topped hut. This garden is meant to be enjoyed!

SHOPPING LIST

Base

- ☐ Painted wooden crate, about 9" x 12" x 5½" high
- ☐ Floral foam to fit in crate
- ☐ Potting soil
- ☐ Assorted faux succulent plants
- ☐ Assorted faux flower stems

Rose

- ☐ Oven bake polymer clay (any color since it will be painted)
- ☐ Large rose cutter for clay
- ☐ Small rose leaf cutter for clay
- ☐ Acrylic clay roller
- ☐ Smooth ball end tool
- ☐ Acrylic paint (green and rose color)

Hut

- ☐ Oven bake polymer clay (any color since it will be painted)
- ☐ Acrylic paint
- ☐ Sheet moss
- ☐ 3 – wood disks

Welcome Sign

- ☐ 3½" x ¼" craft wood picks
- ☐ Acrylic paint (desired colors)

Swing

- ☐ Cotton cording
- ☐ 6 – 4" long twigs
- ☐ 4 – 1" long twigs
- ☐ 1 – 2" long twig

General Supplies

- ☐ Hot glue and glue gun
- ☐ Paintbrushes

TO MAKE THE ROSE HUT GARDEN:

Rose

1. Knead clay until it is soft and pliable; roll out to ⅛" thick. Cut 5 flat flower shapes with the large rose cutter. Create a small clay cone; the base should fit the flower center and be about half the height of one flower petal.

2. Flatten the flower edges with the ball end tool or your fingers.

3. For the flower center, place the clay cone in the center of one flower shape and fold one petal up and around the cone. Skip a petal and fold the next petal up and around the cone. Repeat until all petals are folded up and around the cone.

4. Place the flower center in the center of another clay flower. Fold one petal up and around the center; shape petal as desired. Skip a petal and fold the next petal up and around the center; shape the petal. Skip a petal and fold the next petal up and around the center; shape the petal. Repeat until all petals are folded up and around the center, shaping as desired.

5. Repeat Step 4 with remaining 3 flower shapes.

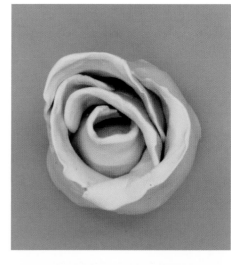

6. Roll clay to ⅛" thick. Cut 4 leaves with small rose leaf cutter.

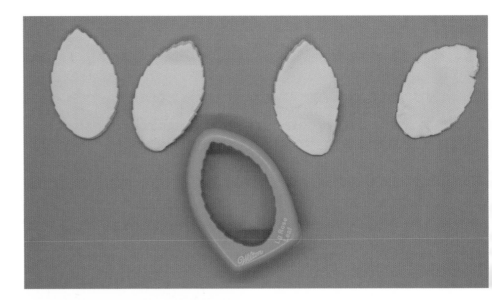

7. Gently press the leaves to the bottom of the rose.

8. Follow the manufacturer's instructions to bake the rose; let cool.

9. Paint the leaves and rose desired colors.

Hut

1. Knead clay until it is soft and pliable; use your hands to roll out and form ¼" thick strands. Twist two strands together to look like a rope.

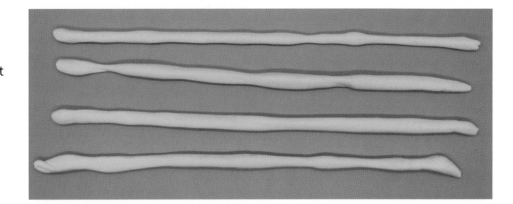

2. Coil and wrap the rope into a circular base about 4" across, adding more twisted ropes as needed. Just smooth the edges together with your fingers.

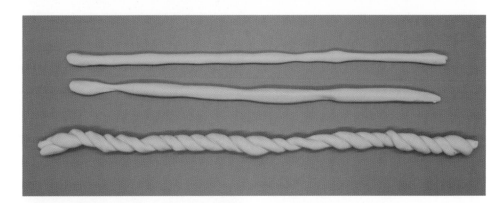

3. To form the hut walls, join a new rope on top of the last rope and smooth into place. Coil the rope around the base one complete circle.

4. Leaving 1½" open for the front, add ropes to build the walls. Wrap the rope ends to the inside.

5. Add ropes to the inside of the wall allowing it to slouch inward. This will narrow the top. Repeat for 3 rope sections.

6. Add a rope section over the front opening. Add 3 more full rope rounds, working on the inside of each round, making the hut more narrow as you continue upward.

7. Follow the manufacturer's instructions to bake the hut; let cool. The clay will slouch into position as it cools and hardens.

8. Paint the hut as desired, making sure to get paint into all the twists and curves of the ropes.

9. Glue the rose to the top of the hut. Glue moss to the hut to fill in empty spaces and to decorate the hut.

10. Stack and glue wood disks together to create a pedestal base for the hut. Glue the hut to the base.

Welcome Sign

1. Arrange wood picks into an arched shape. To hold the sign together, glue 2 picks across the arch at the back and 3 picks across the front.

2. Paint the sign white; let dry. Paint "Welcome to My Garden" and a flower on the sign front.

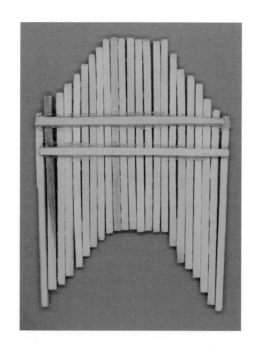

Swing

1. For the swing supports, glue two 4" long twigs together at top in an upside "V" shape. Glue a 1" long twig across the middle. Repeat.

2. Glue three 1" long twigs together side by side; repeat. Cut two pieces of cording each 6" long. Knot each cording pieces at one end. Place both knots between the twig sections and glue sections together.

3. Glue the 2" twig to the tops of the swing supports. Knot the cording to the top twig, adjusting the length so the seat swings.

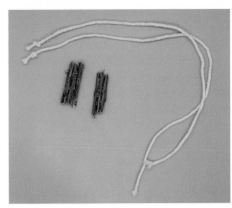

Assembly

1. Trim the foam to fit in the crate, leaving 1" below the handle openings for soil. Cover the foam with soil.

2. Place the hut in one corner. Place the swing and sign near the hut. Add the plants and flower stems to the crate, gently moving the soil as needed.

moss hut garden

Such a sweet little moss hut for the fairies to call home! From the trellis to the tire swing, the fairies have a lovely hideaway tucked away in the greens.

SHOPPING LIST

Base
- ☐ Round wooden box about 12" diameter and 3" high
- ☐ Solid foam disc to fit in box and fill box to ½" below rim (you can stack discs if necessary)
- ☐ Potting soil

Hut
- ☐ 4½" x 5⁄16" wood craft sticks

Roof
- ☐ Heavyweight cardstock
- ☐ Tape

Tire Swing
- ☐ Cotton cording
- ☐ Mini toy tire
- ☐ 5" high Y-shaped twig with one long arm

Flower Arbor
- ☐ 4 – 6" long twigs
- ☐ 9 – 1" long twigs
- ☐ 2 – 3" long gently curved twigs for arbor top
- ☐ Mini faux berry-like flowers

Steps
- ☐ Wood disks of various sizes

Painted Sign
- ☐ River rock large enough to write on
- ☐ White paint marker

General Supplies
- ☐ Fairy figurines
- ☐ River rocks
- ☐ Reindeer moss
- ☐ Dried vines
- ☐ Mini faux flowers
- ☐ Hot glue and glue gun
- ☐ Sandpaper
- ☐ Craft knife

TO MAKE THE MOSS HUT GARDEN:

Base

1. Use sandpaper to rough up one side of several rocks.

2. Glue the rocks to the box side. Glue moss between the rocks. Glue the dried vine to the box, adding bits of moss here and there.

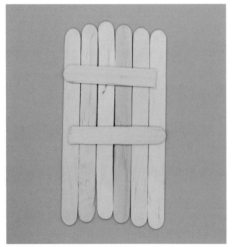

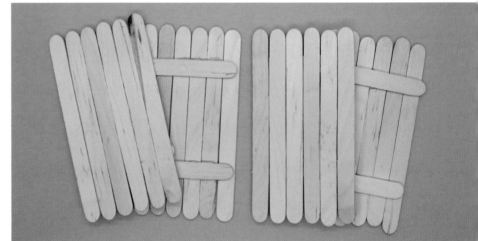

Hut

1. Cut 4 craft sticks in half.

2. For the wall panel, use 2 cut pieces to glue 6 craft sticks together. Make 4 wall panels. Glue the wall panels together. Glue 4 craft sticks to the bottom for anchors.

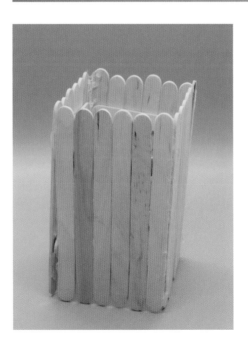

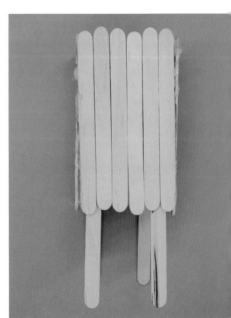

3. Use sandpaper to rough up one side of each rock, then glue rocks to the lower half of the wall panels, stacking about 3-4 rows.

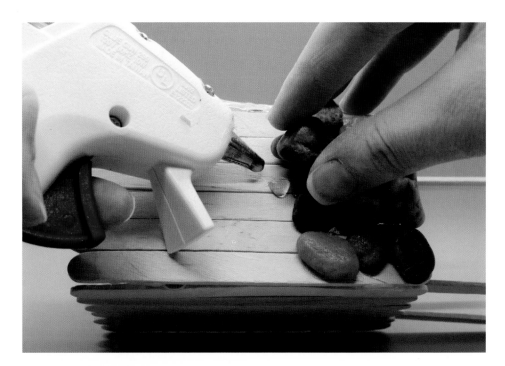

4. Glue moss into the open spaces between rocks and on the uncovered portion of the wall panels.

5. Wrap a few vines around the wall panels, gluing in place as necessary. Glue a few flowers to the wall panels.

Roof

1. Cut a 6" circle from cardstock. Draw a line from the edge to the center; cut along the drawn line.

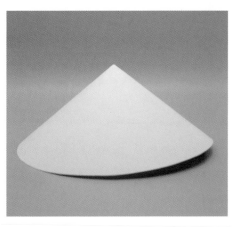

2. Fold the cut circle into a cone shape that will fit over the wall panels; tape the cardstock cone to hold the shape.

3. Glue moss to the cone, completely covering the cardstock. Wrap vines around the roof, gluing as necessary. Glue flowers to the roof.

4. Glue the roof to the top of the wall panels.

Tire Swing

Cut a 6" piece of cotton cording. Tie one end to the tire and the other to the long arm of the Y-shaped twig; trim the excess cording. Glue flowers to the twig.

Flower Arbor

1. For each arbor side, glue two 1" twigs to two 6" twigs. Be sure to leave the bottom 2" of each arbor side clear, as these legs will be inserted into the dirt. Glue three 1" twigs to the 2 curved twigs in the same manner. Glue the curved twigs to the tops of the arbor sides.

2. Glue the berry-like flowers to the top and sides of the arbor. Wrap dried vines around the arbor and glue in place.

Steps

Stack the wooden disks alongside the base to determine how many you need to complete the steps. Starting with the largest at the bottom, glue the disks together in a stair step fashion with approximately ½" of wood showing from the previous step. It's really cute to curve the steps just a bit as they go up. Check them against the box as you glue, so you can determine placement. Fill in the steps with moss and glue on some flowers.

Painted Sign

1. Use sandpaper to rough up one side edge of the river rock. Use the paint marker to write "The Fairies" on the smooth side of the rock.

2. Use sandpaper to rough up one side of 2 smaller river rocks; glue rocks together to form a pedestal. Glue the sign to the pedestal.

Assembly

1. Glue the steps to the box. If needed, add twigs and moss for support. Trim the foam disc to fit in box, leaving ½" below the rim for potting soil. Add potting soil to cover the foam.

2. Placing the hut at back center, insert anchors into foam. Place small wooden disk "stepping stones" on soil leading from the steps to the hut.

3. Insert the tire swing and arbor twigs into the foam. Add plants to the box, gently moving the soil as needed. Fill in with river rocks, placing the painted sign in front of the hut or where desired.

TIP

I used faux succulents for an easy-care, yet great looking, fairy garden.

pinecone hut garden

Walking through the woods and what do you see? There, nestled in the colorful flowers, a simple pinecone hut with a picket fence and a small fire pit. Is this the home of a fairy? Or is someone hoping a fairy will take up residence?

SHOPPING LIST

Base

- [ ] Wooden bowl (my container is 12" diameter x 4" high)
- [ ] Floral foam to fill bowl
- [ ] Potting soil
- [ ] Faux greenery and tall floral stems

Hut

- [ ] Toilet paper tube
- [ ] Tree bark (I used birchwood)
- [ ] 3½" x ¼" craft wood picks
- [ ] 3½" long twigs
- [ ] Pinecones

Fire Pit

- [ ] LED tealight candle
- [ ] Sandpaper
- [ ] 1" long twigs

Fence

- [ ] Floral wire
- [ ] Pliers or wire cutters
- [ ] 3½" x ¼" craft wood picks
- [ ] Tape
- [ ] Dried vines
- [ ] Mini faux flowers

General Supplies

- [ ] River rocks
- [ ] Sheet moss
- [ ] Hot glue and glue gun

TO MAKE THE PINECONE HUT GARDEN:

Hut

1. For the pedestal, glue bark to toilet paper tube, layering to cover the tube. Glue wood picks to bottom for anchors.

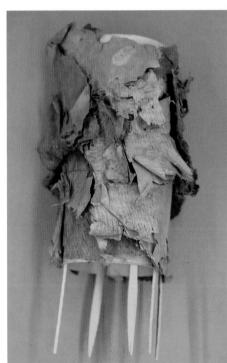

2. For the hut floor, lay 18 wood picks side-by-side. Glue wood picks near the top and bottom as supports. Flip the floor over and glue 2 more wood picks on as supports.

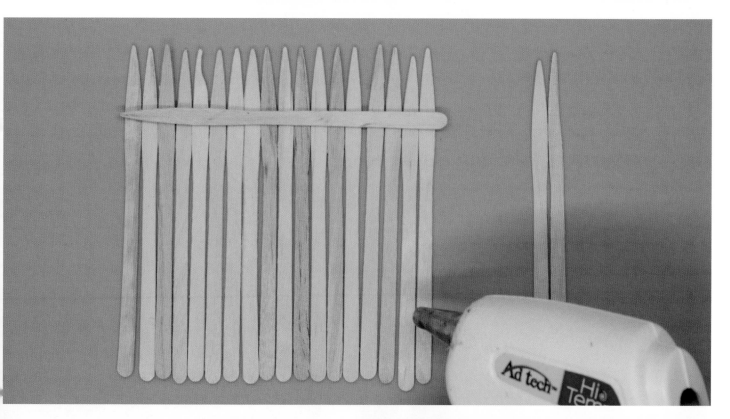

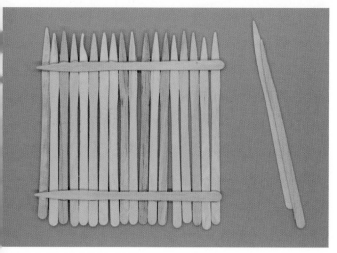

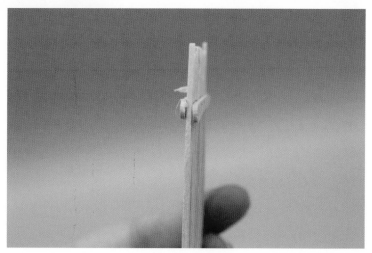

3. For the hut's side and back walls, lay twigs side-by-side until they are about the same width as a wood pick's length. Glue wood picks near the top and bottom as supports. Make 3 walls. Glue the walls to the floor.

4. For the front wall, cut several twigs in half. Lay twigs side-by-side until they are about the same width as a wood pick's length, placing the shorter twigs at the center for the doorway. Glue craft sticks near the top and bottom as supports. Glue the wall to the floor.

5. For the roof, make 2 frames each using 6 wood picks. Glue the frames to the walls, adding a wood pick across front and back for support. Glue pinecone "shingles" to the frames, starting at the bottom and working your way to the top. Glue 3 rows of shingles to the front and back, gluing shingles to the frame and to each other. Add moss to fill in any open spots.

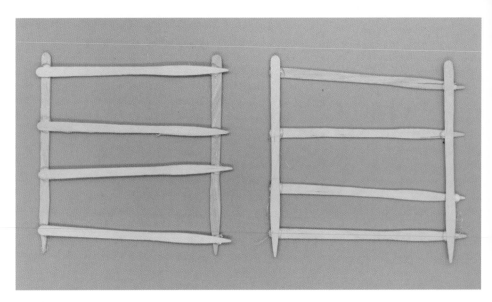

6. Add moss to any open spots on entire hut. Glue the pedestal to the hut bottom.

Fire Pit

1. Use sandpaper to rough up one side of several rocks. Glue the rough side of the rocks to the candle.

2. Layer and glue sticks around candle top. Fill in spaces with moss.

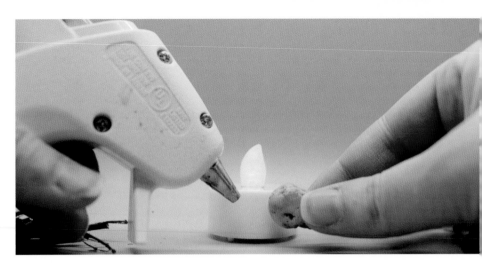

Fence

1. Cut four 20" lengths of floral wire. Twist 2 pieces together 3-5 times at one end. Repeat with remaining wire pieces. Tape the ends to the work surface about 1½" apart. Place a wood pick on the wires, close to the twists. Twist the wires twice each.

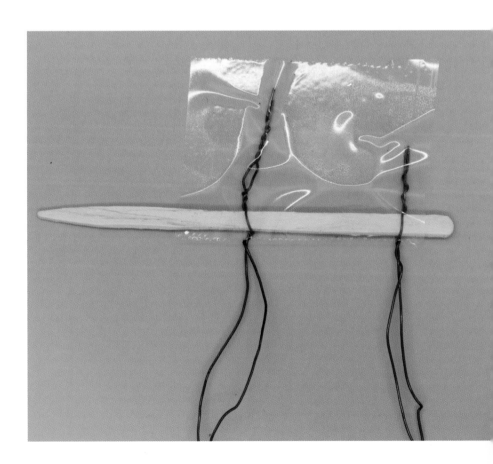

2. Add a new wood pick and twist the wires twice each.

3. Repeat last step until desired length of fence is complete. Twist wire ends and trim wire.

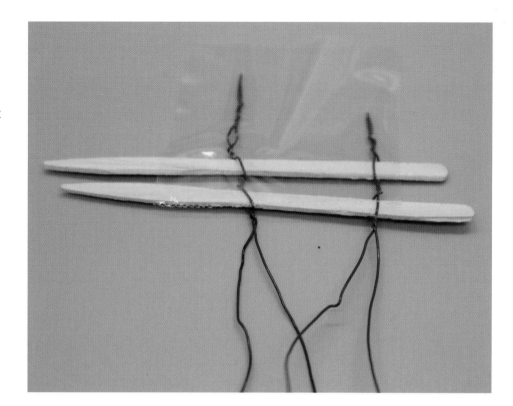

Assembly:

1. Trim the foam to fit in the bowl, leaving 1" below the rim for soil. Cover with potting soil and sheet moss.

2. Insert hut anchors into foam at the back center of bowl. Insert fence into soil around hut. Glue dried vine and mini flowers to fence front and back.

3. Place fire pit on left side. Add river rocks to create garden path. Add plants and floral stems, gently moving moss and soil as needed.

cord house garden

Even fairies need to have a secret get-away spot. An open and airy little house, complete with snuggly leaves and surrounded by colorful mushrooms, is just the place for a peaceful respite. The softly babbling brook enhances the solitude.

SHOPPING LIST

Base

- ☐ Decorative planter about 8" x 12" (I found a vintage planter at a flea market)
- ☐ Multicolored mini pebbles
- ☐ Soil
- ☐ River rocks
- ☐ Floral foam to fit in planter
- ☐ Faux plants

Pennant Banner

- ☐ Scrapbook paper for pennants
- ☐ 2 – 6" long twigs
- ☐ Jute cording

Bridge

- ☐ 2" long twigs about ½" diameter (I used 16 twigs)
- ☐ 2 twigs about 3" long and ½" diameter

Mushrooms

- ☐ Oven bake polymer clay (any color since it will be painted)
- ☐ Acrylic paints in white and desired mushroom cap colors
- ☐ Toothpicks

Welcome Sign

- ☐ 3½" x ¼" craft wood pick
- ☐ 4½" x ⁵⁄₁₆" wood craft stick
- ☐ Acrylic paints in desired colors

Cord House

- ☐ Cotton cording
- ☐ Small round balloon
- ☐ Acrylic paints in desired color
- ☐ Permanent marker
- ☐ Dried leaves for inside house

General Supplies

- ☐ Fairy figurine
- ☐ Mini faux flowers
- ☐ Reindeer moss
- ☐ Craft glue
- ☐ Hot glue and glue gun
- ☐ Paintbrushes

TO MAKE THE CORD HOUSE GARDEN:

Pennant Banner

1. Cut an 8" length of jute cording. Tie one end to each twig (adjust length as needed for space).

2. Fold a piece of scrapbook paper in half and cut small triangles along the folded edge.

3. Wrap the pennants over the cording and glue with craft glue.

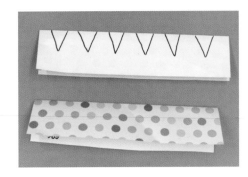

Bridge

1. Hot glue shorter twigs to the longer twigs. On each side, glue shorter twigs to the bottom edge so that the bridge will arch.

2. Add moss and mini flowers to cover empty spaces.

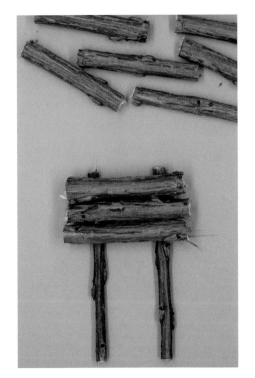

Mushrooms

1. Knead clay until it is soft and pliable. Form the mushroom tops from clay, making both flat and pointy styles. Each should be about ½" x ½".

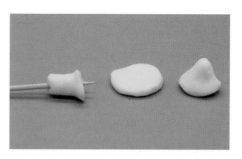

2. Form the mushroom bases. Insert a toothpick through the base, from the bottom up. Place a mushroom top on the toothpick. Smooth the top and base together along the edges to join.

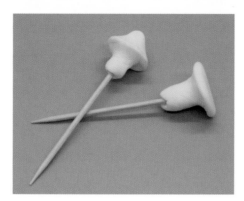

3. Follow the manufacturer's instructions to bake the clay pieces; let cool.

4. Paint the base white and the top a solid color; allow to dry. Add white dots to the top.

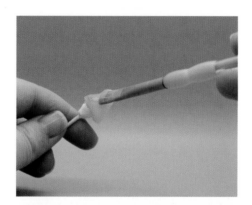
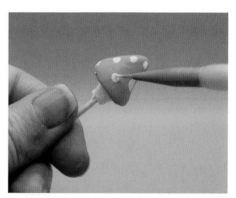

Welcome Sign

1. Break the craft stick on both ends, leaving a 2" piece with rough ends. Paint the sign and add "Welcome" and some flowers.

2. Hot glue the sign to the wood pick.

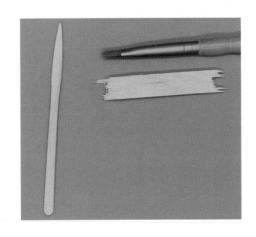

Cord House

1. Blow the balloon up to 6" diameter; knot the end. Use marker to draw a circle for house opening.

2. Using fingers, coat cording with craft glue as you randomly wrap the cord around the balloon. Marker may bleed onto the cord, but it will be painted. Tie a cord to the balloon knot and hang to dry. Once dry, pop and remove the balloon.

3. Paint the house opening.

Assembly

1. Trim the foam fit in the planter, leaving 1" below the rim for soil. Cover the foam with soil. Insert the pennant banner twigs into the foam near the back. Insert the mushroom toothpicks into the foam as desired.

2. Use the mini pebbles to create the "brook." Test fit the bridge over the brook; adjust as necessary. Place river rocks along the brook edges. Place the bridge over the brook.

3. Place the house behind the banner; place leaves and the fairy inside the house. Insert the sign into the foam. Add the plants to the planter, gently moving the soil, rocks and pebbles as needed.

meet kristi Simpson

Inspired by her love of yarn, Kristi Simpson creates crochet, knit, and macramé projects with a fresh and modern touch. The mother of five became hooked on crochet after teaching herself so she could teach her daughter to make a scarf from a "learn to crochet" kit that was a gift.

"I loved it from the beginning!" she says, "I'm amazed that I could take a strand of yarn and create something so useful and pretty! Needless to say, I never stopped!"

She also loves all crafts such as macramé, cardmaking, and scrapbooking.

Look for other Leisure Arts books featuring Kristi's designs at www.leisurearts.com/meet-the-designers/kristi-simpson.html

We have made every effort to ensure that these instructions are accurate and complete. We cannot, however, be responsible for human error, typographical mistakes, or variations in individual work.

Production Team: Technical Writer – Mary Hutchinson; Technical Associate – Sarah J. Green; Senior Graphic Artist – Lora Puls; Graphic Artist – Lori Malkin Ehrlich; Photostylist – Lori Wenger; and Photographer – Jason Masters.

Made in U.S.A.